MODERN ENGLISH PLAYWRIGHTS

MODERN ENGLISH PLAYWRIGHTS

A Short History of the
English Drama from 1825

BY

JOHN W. CUNLIFFE

*Professor of English and Director of the School
of Journalism in Columbia University
in the City of New York*

PUBLISHERS

HARPER & BROTHERS
NEW YORK AND LONDON
1927

TO
"THE HELPERS AND THE SERVERS—
THEY MUST DO THEIR PART TOO,
IF IT IS TO BE OF ANY GOOD."

CONTENTS

PREFACE

From many years' experience of discussing modern literature both in the classroom and in print, I am aware of the provisional character of all judgments upon recent dramatic developments, and the opinions here presented, whether my own or other people's, are submitted with full reservation of the reader's right to re-adjust them to his own standard of values. I hope, none the less, that this connected account of what appears to me one of the most remarkable periods of English dramatic history will be of interest and of use.

I am obliged to the editor of the Series, Professor A. H. Quinn, whose view of recent dramatic developments is very different from mine, not only for the privilege of expressing my own opinions on controversial issues, but for many useful suggestions. I am indebted to Harper & Brothers for the use of copyright material in quotation from the text of recent plays; to Brentano's for permission to quote the excerpts from Bernard Shaw's plays; to Little, Brown and Co. for the citation from Sir Johnston Forbes-Robertson's *A Player under Three Reigns;* to Dodd, Mead and Co. for extracts from William Archer's *Playmaking* and *The Old Drama and the New;* to the Houghton Mifflin Co. for the lines quoted from John Drinkwater's *Abraham Lincoln;* to John W. Luce and Co. for quotations from J. M. Synge's *The Aran Islands* and *The Playboy of the Western World* and from Stanley Houghton's *Hindle Wakes;* to Martin Secker Ltd. for the passages quoted from St. John

Hankin's plays; and to G. P. Putnam's Sons for the passage from Lord Dunsany's *A Night at an Inn.*

Cordial thanks are also offered to the officers of the British Museum and the Bodleian Libraries, the New York Public Library, and the Columbia University Library for their unfailing courtesy and helpfulness. I wish to make special mention of the persevering skill of Mrs. Hitchcock, Librarian of the Columbia Journalism Library, and her staff, in running down for me dates and other elusive details as to which accuracy is a much prized virtue but one not easily attainable in the modern field.

MODERN ENGLISH PLAYWRIGHTS

CHAPTER I

INTRODUCTORY

THE nineteenth century brought the English theatre back to the people and the English people back to the theatre, but it took nearly the whole of the century to complete the reconciliation. In the early years of the Victorian era, an intelligent observer might well have thought that the prospects of the drama had not greatly improved since the Puritans closed the theatres in 1642; the Restoration had re-opened the theatre, but only to the most idle, the most frivolous, and the most debauched class of the nation —the Court and its hangers-on. When the Court became more respectable, the theatre lost its support without gaining that of the solid and industrious middle class which was slowly coming into power. The estrangement of the middle class from the theatre, resting upon a long-established tradition, was encouraged by the conditions under which plays were produced and by the kind of entertainment offered. Up to 1843 the performance of "legitimate" drama was restricted by law to two of the London theatres —Drury Lane and Covent Garden—under letters patent granted by Charles II at the Restoration, reinforced by Sir Robert Walpole's Licensing Act of 1737. But permission to present musical entertainments, partly dramatic in character, could still be obtained from the Lord Chamberlain for smaller theatres which were allowed to open during the summer months when the "patent" houses were closed. The success of the "summer" houses led the regular theatres

The "patent" theatres

1

to extend their winter season and to offer similar entertainments; the minor theatres retaliated by encroaching upon the winter months and the dramatic programmes which were supposed to be the monopoly of the regular houses. The usual bill of the smaller theatres, however, consisted of "pantomimes, ballets, farces, melodramas—all bearing the orthodox title of *burlettas*" with such occasional attractions as tight-rope dancers and performing dogs. The oldest of the minor theatres, Sadler's Wells, presented in 1825 the following programme, which has been preserved in Hone's *Every Day Book:*

The amusements will consist of a romantic tale of mysterious horror and broad grin, never acted, called the *Enchanted Girdles, or Winki the Witch, and the Ladies of Samarchand.* A most whimsical burletta, which sends people home perfectly exhausted from uninterrupted risibility, called *The Lawyer, The Jew, and The Yorkshireman,* with, by request of 75 distinguished families, and a party of 5, that never to be sufficiently praised pantomime, called *Magic in Two Colours, or Fairy Blue and Fairy Red, or Harlequin and the Marble Rock.* It would be perfectly superfluous for any man in his senses to attempt anything more than the mere announcement in recommendation of the above unparalleled representations, so attractive in themselves as to threaten a complete monopoly of the qualities of the magnet; and though the proprietors were to talk nonsense for an hour, they could not assert a more *important truth* than that they possess the only Wells from which you may draw wine, three shillings and sixpence, a full quart. Those whose important avocations prevent their coming at the commencement will be admitted for half price at half-past eight. Ladies and gentlemen who are not judges of the superior entertainments announced are respectfully requested to bring as many as possible with them who are. N. B.—A full moon during the week.

The special attraction at Sadler's Wells at this period was the "aquatic" drama, acted upon a gigantic tank; real ships floated upon real water, and the heroine fell in to be rescued by the hero or a Newfoundland dog. The home of the "equestrian" drama was Astley's Amphitheatre on the south side of the Thames, just across Westminster bridge. It was here that the famous rider Ducrow, celebrated by "Christopher North" in *Noctes Ambrosianæ*, gave his time-honoured injunction to the actors "Cut the cackle and come to the 'osses," adding, "I'll show you how to cut it. You say 'Yield thee, Englishman!' Then you (indicating the other) answer 'Never!' Then you say 'Obstinate Englishman, you die.' Then you both fights. There, that settles the matter; the audience will understand you a deal better, and the poor 'osses won't catch cold while you're jawing." "Cut the cackle

The successful competition of the minor theatres drove the "patent" houses in desperation to similar forms of entertainment, and it was the combination of tight-rope dances with a famous lion-tamer at Drury Lane that led the young Queen Victoria to pay the house the remarkable compliment of two special performances by royal command in 1839. By this time the monopoly of the "patent" houses had become an absurdity, and it was abolished by Act of Parliament in 1843. The extension of the privilege of playing Shakespeare and Sheridan to the smaller theatres was regarded with eager expectance, but only one of them, Sadler's Wells, under the management of Samuel Phelps, made any distinguished use of the opportunity. Whether it was the kind of entertainment offered that drove away the sober and educated sections of the population, or the character of the audience that prescribed the kind of entertainment necessary for financial success, the degradation of the stage in the first half of the nineteenth century is beyond question. Sir Walter Scott, in answer to a suggestion that he might do something for the London stage, could write in 1819: "I do not think the character of the audience in London is such that one could have the least pleasure in pleasing them. One half come to prosecute Queen Victoria at Drury Lane their debaucheries, so openly that it would degrade a bag-nio; another set to snooze off their beef-steaks and port wine; a third are critics of the fourth column of the news-paper; fashion, wit, or literature there is not, and, on the whole, I would far rather write verses for mine honest friend Punch [the street 'Punch and Judy'] and his audience. The only thing that could tempt me to be so silly, would be to assist a friend in such a degrading task, who was to have the whole profit and the shame of it."

Professor Henry Morley

Nearly fifty years later Professor Henry Morley in the Prologue to his *Journal of a London Playgoer from 1851 to 1866* says: "The great want of the stage in our day is an educated public that will care for its successes, honestly inquire into its failures, and make managers and actors feel that they are not dependent for appreciation of their efforts on the verdict that comes of the one mind divided into fragments between Mr. Dapperwit in the stalls, Lord Froth in the side-boxes, and Pompey Doodle in the gallery. The playgoer who would find in our London theatres a dramatic literature, in which England is rich beyond all other nations, fitly housed, may be indignant at much that he sees in them. But what if Doodle, Dapperwit and Froth do clap their hands at pieces which are all leg and no brains; in which the male actor's highest ambition is to caper, slide, and stamp with the energy of a street-boy on a cellar-flap, the actress shows plenty of thigh, and the dialogue, running entirely on the sound of words, hardly admits that they have any use at all as signs of thought? Whose fault is it that the applauders of these dismal antics sit so frequently as umpires in the judgment of dramatic literature?"

Yet outside the theatre there were the multitudinous readers of Thackeray and Dickens, Charlotte Brontë and

4

George Eliot, Anthony Trollope and Thomas Hardy, the public which was brought, somewhat reluctantly, to appreciate the poetry of Tennyson and Browning. It was a public of marked prejudices and of limited sympathies, but it was not uneducated or unintelligent beyond the possibility of artistic appreciation. The theatre was neither respected nor respectable; people of education and refinement found nothing to break down their inherited prejudices save the occasional revival of a Shakespearean masterpiece by a leading actor, or the still rarer performance of Goldsmith's *She Stoops to Conquer*, or Sheridan's *School for Scandal*. Poets were called upon, as Browning was by Macready, to "write me a play and save me from going to America," but the result disappointed alike the audience, the actor, and the dramatist. The reasons for the failure are sufficiently obvious; the poets were held fast by the romantic tradition. They were still writing for the Elizabethan stage and chose subjects which permitted treatment in long, rhetorical speeches, and made no appeal to the interests of a modern audience. They did not know the theatre and they did not adapt their plays to the modern picture stage. Playwrights and actors were ill paid, and gained nothing in public esteem to make up for the lack of pecuniary reward. When Browning attended incognito the performance of one of his plays, he was bewildered by the question of the man in the next seat, "Is this Browning the author of *Romeo and Juliet?*"—a reference to a burlesque of the Shakespearean tragedy then popular. Undeterred by early failures, Browning made repeated attempts to capture the stage, but had ultimately to content himself with writing closet drama. Charming as some of the plays are for subtlety of characterization and occasional beauty of expression, the Browning admirer is bound to acknowledge that they have no theatrical life in them; and the same is to be said of the later attempts of Lord Tennyson and Stephen Phillips, in which fluent and graceful versification and gorgeous settings were offered as substitutes for plot and passion.

Another depressing element, arising perhaps inevitably out of the degradation of the drama, was the absence of any real criticism. The romantic criticism of Coleridge, Hazlitt and Lamb dealt with the Shakespearean drama as literature, but made little reference to the qualities even of these plays for dramatic representation. Indeed, Lamb wrote of Lear: "The Lear of Shakespeare cannot be acted. The contemptible machinery by which they mimic the storm which he goes out in, is not more inadequate to represent the horrors of the real elements than any actor can be to represent Lear; they might more easily propose to personate the Satan of Milton upon a stage, or one of Michael Angelo's terrible figures. The greatness of Lear is not in corporal dimension, but in intellectual; the explosions of his passion are terrible as a volcano; they are storms turning up and disclosing to the bottom that sea, his mind, with all its vast riches. It is his mind that is laid bare. This case of flesh and blood seems too insignificant to be thought on; even as he himself neglects it. On the stage we see nothing but corporal infirmities and weakness, the impotence of rage; while we read it, we see not Lear, but we are Lear."

The realization that Shakespeare's plays were written to be acted and were adapted to the stage for which they were written, was not reached till nearly the end of the nineteenth century, and has been noted as a contribution to the better appreciation of the theatre and its possibilities. The contemporary criticism of the plays actually

No real criticism

put upon the boards was conventional and perfunctory until the last quarter of the century, when William Archer and Bernard Shaw began to write for the London press. The mid-century critics cannot be entirely blamed for saying nothing worth while, for they had little that it was worth while to criticize.

The sensational melodramas of Lord Lytton (Sir Edward Lytton Bulwer) and of Dion Boucicault were popular, but they hardly offered material for serious discussion, although they may serve us very well as examples of the dramatic fare of the period. Boucicault was the Scribe of the English and American stage with 124 dramas to his credit. Born in Dublin in 1822 (his real name was Dionysius Boursecault) he leapt into fame before he was nineteen by the production of his first comedy, *London Assurance*, at Covent Garden Theatre. After making other plays, mainly borrowings from the French, some of them successes, some failures, for the London theatres, Boucicault at the age of thirty took to the stage as an actor and almost immediately transferred his activities to New York, where his earlier plays were already popular. More French adaptations followed—including *The Corsican Brothers*—and at the end of the 'fifties Boucicault had become the most conspicuous English dramatist, dividing his energies between London and New York. The success of the new Winter Garden Theatre season of 1859-60 was *The Octoroon*, Boucicault's first drama of American life, in which he himself took the part of the faithful Indian chief, Wah-no-tee. Attired in complete war paint and fully armed, Wah-no-tee at the end of the play confronts the villainous overseer, M'Closky, who with a bowie knife in his hand is trying to escape after setting fire to the steamer.

Dion Boucicault

The Octoroon

7

"Stand clear," cries M'Closky. "You won't—die, fool!" and we have the following stage direction:

> Thrusts at him—Wah-no-tee, with his tomahawk, strikes the knife out of his hand; M'Closky starts back; Wah-no-tee throws off his blanket, and strikes at M'Closky several times, who avoids him; at last he catches his arm, and struggles for the tomahawk, which falls; a violent struggle and fight take place, ending with the triumph of Wah-no-tee, who drags M'Closky along the ground, takes up the knife and stabs him repeatedly; George enters, bearing Zoe in his arms—all the Characters rush on—noise increasing —the steam vessel blows up—grand Tableau, and Curtain.

This was presented in London in 1861 as a picture of "life in Louisiana" and kept the stage up to the end of the nineteenth century, but Boucicault's more permanent reputation rests upon the series of Irish dramas beginning with *The Colleen Bawn*, first put on the New York stage in 1860, and during the following season acted by Boucicault and his wife (Agnes Robertson) 360 times at London and provincial theatres. When *The Colleen Bawn* was revived at the London Princess's Theatre in 1896, it attained the dignity of a three column notice by Bernard Shaw, then dramatic critic for the *Saturday Review* (afterwards included in Volume I of his *Dramatic Opinions and Essays*). Naturally the main part of the article is more about the stage Irishman than about the play, but the following paragraph throws some light on the stage conditions then prevailing:

The Colleen Bawn [margin note]

> I have lived to see *The Colleen Bawn* with real water in it; and perhaps I shall live to see it some day with real Irishmen in it, though I doubt if that will heighten its popularity much. The real water lacks the translucent cleanliness of the original article, and destroys the illusion of Eily's drowning and Myles na Coppaleen's header to a quite amazing degree; but the spectacle of the two performers taking a call before the curtain, sopping wet,

and bowing with a miserable enjoyment of the applause, is one which I shall remember with a chuckle whilst life remains.

Even more popular than *The Colleen Bawn* was its successor *Arrah-na-Pogue*, first put on in 1864-5 in Dublin and London, and speedily reproduced in "all the principal cities of England, America, and Australia." The great scene is the escape of the hero Shaun from his condemned cell to "music, mostly tremolo." The stage direction reads further, *"Wall descends,"* and as the wall descends, the audience has a glimpse of Shaun climbing up it, amid the ivy. *"All is worked down. Gas up."* We see the heroine (played by Mrs. Boucicault) singing on a set bank, unconscious that Shaun (Boucicault himself) is climbing up to her. Michael Feeny ("first Low Comedy"), maddened by Arrah's rejection of his suit, interposes to hurl Shaun to his doom, but Shaun opportunely seizes him by the ankles, and it is Feeny, not Shaun, who falls into the lake a hundred feet below. At that very moment, Shaun's pardon arrives, and all ends happily, for Feeny is none the worse for his wetting. *Arrah-na-Pogue* was given in London by amateurs for charity in 1893, but it survived in New York (after an absence of twenty years) till 1903 and in Philadelphia till 1908, as given by Andrew Mack, "the singing comedian," supported by a mixed chorus of "comely girls and stalwart men," who sang "The Wearing of the Green" and other Irish songs, some of them new, and one of them Mack's own composition. Mack took his company round the world, and in Australia and New Zealand had an enthusiastic reception.

A French version of *Arrah-na-Pogue* held the stage for 140 nights in Paris, and when in 1865 Joseph Jefferson reached London on his way back from his Australian tour,

Arrah-na-Pogue

it was naturally to Boucicault that he turned to make over an old play in his repertory, *Rip van Winkle*. It was Boucicault's version that was presented by Jefferson to the London public in that year and was "accepted without hesitation as one of the finest works of modern dramatic art." As the piece had been re-written by Jefferson's half-brother, Charles Burke, and made over by Jefferson himself before he handed the MS. to Boucicault, this play seems to belong to the history of the American drama rather than here. Boucicault wrote many plays for London theatres and even took a lease of Covent Garden with a stage-struck English peer, who lost many thousands of pounds by the transaction, "but the spectacular display was admitted to be the finest ever seen in London." After twelve years in England Boucicault returned to New York and made his home there, paying only occasional visits to England, until his death in 1890; in that year he was still writing plays and one of his most recent efforts was on the stage, but of this later period the only drama that *The Shaughraun* seems to call for mention is *The Shaughraun* (1874), in which Boucicault, both at Drury Lane, London, and at Wallack's Theatre, New York, took the part of Conn, "the soul at every Fair, the Life of every Funeral, the First Fiddle at all Weddings." Conn is the centre of the humorous business of the play, but its plot is concerned with the fortunes of a gallant young Fenian, Robert Ffolliott, who has returned to Sligo after escaping from penal servitude in Australia. An equally gallant young Englishman, Captain Molineux (played at Drury Lane by that excellent English actor, Terriss) is directed to capture him, and in searching for him falls in love at first sight with his sister, Claire Ffolliott; all are ignorant that "Her Majesty has been pleased to extend a full pardon to the

Fenian prisoners, but as Robert Ffolliott has effected his escape, the pardon will not extend to him unless he should reconstitute himself a prisoner." Ffolliott, taking refuge at Father Dolan's house and being tracked there by Captain Molineux, unwittingly fulfils the condition of his own pardon by giving himself up in order to save the priest from telling a lie—a situation used half a century later by Galsworthy in *Escape*. The two villains of the play, to whom alone the fact of Ffolliott's pardon is known, plot to rob him of the advantage by inducing him to break prison and be picked up by a boat off the coast. They intend to shoot him as he escapes, but hit the Shaughraun by mistake. Conn is only slightly wounded, but he feigns death and is so able to assist at his own wake—one of the most popular scenes of the play. After many vicissitudes, the villains are defeated, Ffolliott's pardon is discovered, his sister accepts Captain Molineux, and the Shaughraun is united to the girl of his heart, the audience being appealed to for surety that he will give up drinking, poaching and all the merry tricks that have endeared him in the course of the action. Boucicault's son Aubrey revived the play in 1896, taking his father's part, and in his hands it kept the stage for some years. In 1922 it was made into a movie under the title *My Wild Irish Rose*, and the films may be still keeping Boucicault's memory green.

Among the other plays which kept the stage, with dwindling respect, might be mentioned *Virginius* (1820) and *The Hunchback* (1832) by Sheridan Knowles; the latter was revived by Viola Allen in 1902, and in the earlier years of this century James O'Neill was still playing *Virginius*, outside of New York and to diminishing audiences. Even longer lived were Lord Lytton's early Victorian melo- Lord dramas, *The Lady of Lyons* (1838) and *Richelieu* (1839). Lytton

11

Of the former the London *Times* records a successful revival at the Scala in 1919, and in 1918 *Richelieu* still formed part of the repertory of Robert Mantell. But at the revival of 1898 by Kyrle Bellew and Mrs. Brown Potter, the London *Daily Chronicle* spoke of *The Lady of Lyons* as "that sentimental product of a bygone age," and the *Illustrated London News* dismissed it as "preposterous and tawdry rubbish, with its tedious rhodomontade and its banal insincerity." In connection with the somewhat earlier revival by E. H. Sothern and Virginia Harned the New York *Evening Post* described the play as a brilliant imposture, welcome to the hardened theatregoer for its many pleasant associations in spite of its bombast and gush, its shady morality, its shallowness, extravagance, and utter artificiality. But for the half century after its first production by Macready at the Theatre Royal, Covent Garden, in 1838, *The Lady of Lyons* was the best known work of its kind and constantly on the boards. The veteran Victorian actor, Henry Howe, in the course of his career embodied in turn every male part the drama contains, beginning with young Major Desmoulins, "the third officer," and finishing up with old Deschappelles. One remembers that Sir Henry Irving was very impressive as the old Richelieu and less effective as the young Claude Melnotte. It hardly seems worth while to recall the extravagance of the plot or the absurdities of the dialogue. A few lines from the reconciliation scene of *The Lady of Lyons* will be sufficient as a sample:

The Lady of Lyons

PAULINE

Oh!

My father, you are saved—and by my husband!
Ah! blessed hour! (*she embraces Melnotte*)

12

INTRODUCTORY

MELNOTTE

Yet you weep still, Pauline!

PAULINE

But on thy breast—*these* tears are sweet and holy!

M. DESCHAPPELLES

You have won love and honour nobly, sir!

MME. DESCHAPPELLES

                    I am astonished!
Who, then, is Colonel Morier?

DAMAS

                  You behold him!

MELNOTTE

Morier no more after this happy day!
I would not bear again my father's name
Till I could deem it spotless! The hour's come!
Heaven smiled on conscience! As the soldier rose
From rank to rank, how sacred was the fame
That cancell'd crime, and raised him nearer thee!

MME. DESCHAPPELLES

A colonel and a hero! Well, that's something!
He's wondrously improved! (*crosses to him*) I wish
                you joy, sir!

MELNOTTE

Ah! the same love that tempts us into sin,
If it be true love, works out its redemption!
And he who seeks repentance for the past
Should woo the Angel Virtue in the future.

(*Curtain*)

13

If these were the masterpieces of the early and mid-Victorian drama, it is difficult to conceive how bad it may have been at its worst, but the reminiscences of Sir Johnston Forbes-Robertson, *A Player under Three Reigns*, give us some idea of the enormities of which it was sometimes capable. Even in the palmy days of the Lyceum, London's leading theatre, in 1879, the company of which Forbes-Robertson was then a member, produced a serious drama called *Zilla or the Scar on the Wrist*, of which he gives the following account:

A Victorian horror

How intricate and disjointed the plot was, may be gathered from the fact that one of the actors, J. H. Barnes, then known as "Handsome Jack", asked me at the third or fourth rehearsal what the play was about. I told him I did not know; this information appeared to give him much relief! The whole company was terribly in earnest, but, on the first night, whatever we said or did was received by pit, gallery, boxes and stalls with shouts of laughter. One of the characters, played by Frank Tyars, was supposed to be slain in the middle of the second act, and there the body lay a long time while other matters were toward. At last the dead man had the scene to himself, upon which, to the amazement of the audience, he rose and uttered a fatal line. "Ha! a light strikes in upon me, I see it all!" "Do you, b'God?" said a voice from the gallery! . . .

During the progress of the play I had to rescue the heroine from the villain's castle, and to do so it was necessary to climb to a high window and carry her through. Now the heroine was playing a dual rôle, a princess and a gipsy, which entailed many rapid changes of costume, and when I dropped with her on the other side of the scene, I found myself in utter darkness caused by some flats having been adjusted immediately under the window at the back, that the lady might change at once from the princess to the gipsy. Protesting voices of mistress and maid came out from the gloom, saying, "Go away, you can't stay here, go away." But there was no going away, as the screens had been firmly tied together and to the back of the scene, the stage hands having

14

left no way for me to escape. I became vaguely conscious that the virgin princess was being stripped, and was much embarrassed by the indignant voices, now growing more insistent, "You cannot remain here; how dare you, etc." At last one of the stage hands realized my highly improper situation, and made an opening for me to slip through.

The gipsy, I need hardly say, had to die before the end of the play, but in order to be able to change to the princess to finish the piece, she, surrounded by her weeping friends, sweetly passed away on a couch, the back of which was so arranged that she might be tipped out, and a very obvious waxen figure take her place. Unfortunately the carpenters had failed to join the end of her couch with the wings, the result being that the poor lady was seen escaping on her hands and knees from the back of the couch to the wings, to the great delight of the audience.

In the last act some important title-deeds had been hidden in a well-bucket hanging very conspicuously in the centre of the market-place. I, as the good genius of the play, was hunting for these title-deeds, and looking for them in even more unlikely places than in the bucket, when a voice from the front shouted: "For Heaven's sake, Robertson, look in the bucket and finish the piece!"

We can hardly be surprised that George Henry Lewes, a diligent student of the contemporary drama in the 'sixties and 'seventies, finding the critic's office "something of a sinecure" in London, went off to see what he could find on the Continent—without receiving much encouragement. He accounted for the universal degradation of the stage, as it appeared to him, as follows (*On Actors and Acting*, Chapter XIII):

George Henry Lewes

The Drama is everywhere in Europe and America rapidly passing from an Art into an Amusement; just as of old it passed from a religious ceremony into an Art. Those who love the Drama cannot but regret the change, but all must fear that it is inevitable when they reflect that the stage is no longer the amusement of the cultured few, but the amusement of the uncultured and miscultured masses, and has to provide larger and lower appetites with food. For one playgoer who can appreciate the beauty of a verse, the delicate humour of a conception, or the exquisite adaptation of means to ends which give ease and harmony to a work of art, there are hundreds, who, insensible to such delights, can appreciate a parody, detect a pun, applaud a claptrap phrase of sentiment, and be exhilarated by a jingle and a dance; for one who can recognize, and recognizing, can receive exquisite pleasure from fine acting, thousands can appreciate costumes, bare necks, and "powerful" grimace; thus the mass, easily pleased, and liberally paying for the pleasure, rules the hour.

Matthew Arnold

Matthew Arnold, writing a few years later (1879), says: "In England we have no drama at all. Our vast society is not homogeneous enough, not sufficiently united, even any large portion of it, in a common view of life, a common ideal capable of serving as basis for a modern English Drama." Even in the 'eighties, in spite of the advent of Jones and Pinero, things did not immediately improve to any marked extent. H. G. Wells recalls in *The World of William Clissold* the days of the late 'eighties and early 'nineties, when he and his hero were in their early twenties and Bernard Shaw was still merely an unsuccessful novelist, better known as a pamphleteer and musical critic; his recollections take form (in 1926) as follows:

H. G. Wells

Those were the absurd days of the British theatre; Barrie and Shaw had yet to dawn upon us; even the mockery of Wilde's *Importance of Being Earnest* had not relieved the pressure of the well-made play, and two leaden masters, Henry Arthur Jones and Pinero, to whom no Dunciad has ever done justice, produced large, slow, pretentious three-act affairs that were rather costume shows than dramas, with scenery like the advertisements of fashionable resorts, the reallest furniture and the unreallest passions and morals it is possible to conceive.

Perhaps there is a touch of malicious exaggeration in Wells's review of the past; but such a sober critic as the late A. B. Walkley of the London *Times* says in *Drama and Life:* "It is impossible to think of the early Victorian theatre without a yawn, so 'unidea'd' was it, so ephemeral, so paltry and jejune. One shrinks from dwelling on this tedious theme." It was not until after the turn of the century (1904, to be exact) that Walkley was able to be a little more cheerful: "There is a small minority of the playgoing public which shows symptoms of discontent. Its artistic conscience, if not deeply stirred, is, at any rate gently pricked. It signs manifestoes, writes to the newspapers, and in other futile ways gives vent to its suspicions that something ought to be done. But what precisely ought to be done nobody knows. Meanwhile the theatres, music-halls in everything but name and an atmosphere of tobacco-smoke, have it all their own way. The vast majority of the public takes its theatrical amusement, as it takes its newspaper information, in snippets. It is a public without patience, without the capacity for sustained attention, and, like Lady Teazle when she married Sir Peter, it has no taste. To speak of the drama as an art to such a public as this is to talk a language which it does not understand, and has no inclination to learn. *Vox clamantis in deserto.*"

A. B. Walkley

It is evident that the depressing conditions outlined above prevailed through the greater part of the nineteenth century and were not entirely overcome at the end of it. About midway in the Victorian era T. W. Robertson made a valiant effort to provide the public with dramatic fare of a light and wholesome character—an effort important enough to demand fuller notice in the next chapter, but this was almost a false dawn, it faded so quickly. It took a long time to dispel the atmosphere or disrepute and con-

T. W. Robertson

tempt in which the theatre was enveloped. The efforts of Irving and Tennyson, though they did little or nothing toward the revival of modern English drama, helped to make the theatre respectable, and the efforts of John Hare, Charles Wyndham, the Bancrofts and the Kendals, were similarly helpful in this regard, especially when their respectability was duly recognized by the bestowal of knighthoods. "Mrs. Kendal," says H. Burton Baker, the historian of the London stage, "was proficient from top to toe; equally at home in the brightest comedy and the deepest pathos of domestic drama, though not in the poetic. Yet this does not quite explain the secret of her popularity; it is rather that she is the representative of all the proprieties of private life, the wife, the mother, the champion— with a very loud trumpet—of the respectabilities; in fine, it is as the matron of the British drama that the *pater* and *mater familias* of the middle classes especially patronize her, rather than for her talent."

The influence of the popular and innocuous operas of Gilbert and Sullivan told in the same direction. Gilbert is on record as saying: "When Sullivan and I determined to work together, the burlesque stage was in a very unclean state. We made up our minds to do all in our power to wipe out the grosser element, never to let an offending word escape our characters, and never to allow a man to appear as a woman or *vice versa*." With the exception of objections to *Ruddigore* on account of its title (for reasons which may mystify a modern reader) and to *The Mikado* on account of its supposed international inopportuneness, Gilbert succeeded in keeping clear of the rocks and quicksands of Victorian prejudice, but the dangers were there and they were not easy to get by, much less to overcome. When the manager of the first Gilbert and Sullivan opera

Gilbert and Sullivan

engaged George Grossmith for the first production, that popular comic entertainer said: "Look at the risks I am running. If I fail I don't believe the Young Men's Christian Association will ever engage me again, because I have appeared on the stage, and my reputation as a comic singer to religious communities will be lost for ever!" Apparently this objection was quite serious, for Grossmith asked three guineas a week extra as insurance against the risk mentioned, although he was persuaded to forego it after the manager had treated him to an unusually good luncheon.

From all these considerations it is obvious that the revival of English drama in the nineteenth century was a task of enormous difficulty, and it is not surprising to find that the earlier efforts were tentative and compromising in character. *The Second Mrs. Tanqueray* may appear to the present generation neither particularly skilful from a technical point of view, nor particularly courageous as a discussion of a social problem, but when it was first produced in 1893 there was a hot debate as to whether it was "the greatest play of the century" or "the most immoral production that has ever disgraced the English stage." It would be easy to dismiss it as neither, but we cannot arrive at an understanding of the masterpieces of English drama in the twentieth century without due consideration of the pioneer work done in the nineteenth, which made the masterpieces possible.

The Second Mrs. Tanqueray

The social prejudices against the theatre in the Victorian era were strongly entrenched, arising partly from the past history of the theatre itself, partly from the prevailing Puritanism of the English middle class, then at the height of its social and political influence. There was little, either by way of pecuniary reward or of public esteem, to sers" or "cup and saucer" drama, which dealt with every-day life in the language of the day.

The first and most obvious reform came precisely from the actors in this despised "trousers" or "cup and saucer" drama. Browning and Tennyson, Swinburne and Stephen Phillips were all on the wrong track; they were harking backward to the Elizabethan age, not dealing with the present or looking forward to the future. The romantic drama, resting on its claim of appealing to the imagination, could content itself with tawdry scenery and shabby dresses, belonging to any period or to none. The actors in the trouser drama insisted on having good trousers, well cut and well pressed; they insisted that doors should have handles, that windows should open, and that the furniture in a scene representing a gentleman's drawing-room should not look as if it came out of a third-rate back office. The equipment of modern comedies with dignified and refined settings led to a similar improvement in the staging of the romantic and the Shakespearean drama. Henry Irving won fame by his Shakespearean spectacles and his example was followed by Beerbohm Tree and others on both sides of the Atlantic. They did a great deal for the stage, but very little for the drama. Irving was a great producer, a great stage manager, a keen psychologist and a considerable Shakespearean critic, but not a great actor, and not really interested in the development of the drama as an art in touch with modern conditions and expressing the national consciousness. The plays he put on were almost without exception great spectacles, Shakespearean or other, or romantic melodrama. When Henry Arthur Jones was asked why he did not write a play for Irving, he said, "Irving does not want a dramatist around his theatre." There is a touch of personal bitterness in the remark, but

That every boy and every gal
  That's born into the world alive
Is either a little Liberal
  Or else a little Conservative,
    Fal, lal, la!

The House of Lords comes equally under the lash. The
Duke and Duchess of Plaza-Toro may be described as
Grandees of Spain, but their ways of getting on were not
(and are not) unknown in London:

DUKE

I sit, by selection,
Upon the direction
  Of several Companies' bubble—
As soon as they're floated
I'm freely bank-noted—
  I'm pretty well paid for my trouble!

DUCHESS

I write letters blatant
On medicines patent—
  And use any other you mustn't—
And vow my complexion
Derives its perfection
  From somebody's soap—which it doesn't!

In a time of confident patriotism, Gilbert had the
courage to bring this conventional sentiment under the
fire of ridicule,—indirectly in *The Mikado:*

But if patriotic sentiment is wanted
  I've patriotic ballads cut and dried;
For where'er our country's banner may be planted,
  All other local banners are defied!
Our warriors, in serried ranks assembled,
  Never quail—or they conceal it if they do—
And I shouldn't be surprised if nations trembled
  Before the mighty troops of Titipu!

Similarly with direct reference to his own country in *H. M. S. Pinafore*, in which the hero's boast, "I am an Englishman" is re-echoed:

> For he might have been a Roosian
> A French, or Turk, or Proosian,
>   Or perhaps Itali-an!
> But in spite of all temptations
> To belong to other nations,
>   He remains an Englishman!
>   Hurrah!
> For the true-born Englishman!

Lightly as these popular ditties were heard, hummed, and sung by the Victorian middle class which the Gilbert and Sullivan operas had brought back to the theatre, the public was not so unintelligent, or so hidebound in its prejudices, as not to catch a gleam of the writer's deeper intention. When the younger generation scoffs at Victorian conventionality, smugness and hypocrisy, it is well to remember that the Victorians listened with good humour and applause to these outspoken criticisms of their weaknesses and follies. It is a long cry from W. S. Gilbert to Bernard Shaw, but the earlier satirist had made a beginning; first by securing the attendance of a middle-class audience at the theatre, and then by winning their approval, he had opened the way for the more profound criticism of national life and character on the stage by his more richly gifted successor.

III. HENRY ARTHUR JONES (1851-   )

When Henry Arthur Jones visited the United States in 1906, he met an American millionaire and bibliophile who laid before him on the table three little books—first editions of *The Rivals*, *The School for Scandal*, and *She Stoops to* Conquer, with the remark, "That's all the harvest of your British drama for the last two hundred years." The American millionaire was a little out of his count, but if he had put back the final date of observation by a dozen years or so, he would not have been far from the truth, though he might still have been thought lacking in politeness to his guest, to say nothing of contemporary dramatists. Jones wrote "a great drama" in 1867, and produced his first play at Exeter in 1878. But the time of these early productions and the conditions of the drama at the time must not be lost sight of. Jones's own remark to Barrett H. Clark is apposite: "Don't forget that when I began it was the day of Robertson and H. J. Byron. They were my only models." Nor were the personal circumstances of Jones's early life at all favourable to dramatic production. The son of a Buckinghamshire farmer, he had a brief education at a local Grammar School, went into business in the North of England at 13, and earned his living as a commercial traveller until he was 30. He gives a striking picture of the alien conditions under which he began to interest himself in dramatic composition. "I became a dramatist because I couldn't help it. I was born in the country among the strictest people, who thought that dancing and playgoing were the devil's own work. In my boyhood I never saw a play or heard any talk about such subjects. I never was in a theatre until I was 18 years old, but two years before that, all alone and discouraged, I had written a great drama of my own."

The success of that once popular melodrama *The Silver King* (1882), done in collaboration with Henry Herman, released Jones from the trammels of business and definitely established his position as a dramatist, but it cannot be considered seriously as a work of art, and was not so considered by our author. He began about this time a series of essays and lectures which were published in volume form in 1895 under the title, *The Renascence of the English Drama*. In 1884, again in collaboration with Mr. Herman, Jones attempted to turn Ibsen's *A Doll's House* into a "sympathetic play" in an adaptation to mid-Victorian tastes called *Breaking a Butterfly*—a performance the adapters would, no doubt, be glad to forget. Jones's work at this time shows little trace of Ibsen's influence, but it is interesting to notice the momentary contact.

Saints and Sinners

In this same year 1884 Jones made an attempt at serious drama in *Saints and Sinners*, published in 1891 (after the passage of the American Copyright Act which protected English authors from American performances of their plays without payment of royalties) with a preface in which Jones deplored the decay of the British drama, and pointed the way to better things by insisting that playwriting should be not merely "the art of sensational and spectacular illusion," but "mainly and chiefly the art of representing English life." *Saints and Sinners* was a gallant but not altogether successful attempt to put these principles into practice. Its inspiration probably came not so much from Ibsen as from George Eliot's studies of English middle-class life, which were at the time exceedingly popular. Matthew Arnold was interested by the play's attack on "the middle-class fetish," and the unsympathetic representation of Puritan morality provoked a discussion to which the author himself contributed in an article in the *Nineteenth Century*. The play was "hooted" by the first-night audience, "condemned by nearly all the London press," and quickly withdrawn. Jones's own account is that he was so discouraged that he weakly sold himself to the "dull devil of spectacular melodrama to which he remained a bondslave for many years." To a modern reader, *Saints and Sinners* will appear fearfully sentimental and melodramatic, and even Jones's admiring American editor, Clayton Hamilton, stamps it as "old fashioned and unquestionably crude," but Jones should be given credit for his good intentions, and a well meant effort as early as 1884 is worthy of record.

The melodramas which followed need no further condemnation than the author himself has given them, but one cannot help deploring the loss of the opportunity of which Jones was himself conscious. The time was ripe for change. Ibsen, first introduced to the British public in a *Fortnightly Review* article by Edmund Gosse in 1873, began to appear in translation in 1876, and the cheap little volumes of the Camelot Classics containing his plays in English had a wide circulation in the later 'eighties and early 'nineties. William Archer, who had begun a lifelong career of able and intelligent work as a dramatic critic in 1879 on the *London Figaro*, in that year published his translation of *A Doll's House;* in 1880 his version of *Pillars of Society* was produced at the Gaiety Theatre. "As I look back to 'seventy-nine and the early 'eighties," he reflected some forty years later, "I confess I am puzzled to conceive how anyone with the smallest pretension to intelligence could in those years seriously occupy himself with the English theatre;" but at the time he was sufficiently aware of the opportunity presented, not only to devote his energies to dramatic criticism and translation, but to collaborate with Bernard Shaw (as early as 1885) on the play which afterwards developed into *Widowers' Houses.* Shaw's *Quintessence of Ibsen* was published in 1891, and the same year *Ghosts* was privately

Ibsen's plays in England

performed at the Independent Theatre in London to the dismay and disgust of the older critics. But it was not Jones but Pinero who swung into the new current of opinion with *The Second Mrs. Tanqueray* in 1893.

The Case of Rebellious Susan Jones followed in 1894 with *The Case of Rebellious Susan*, more than capably presented at the Criterion Theatre by Wyndham and Mary Moore. Though the author's preface indicates that the "case" presented was "perhaps a tragedy" rather than a light comedy, the dramatist makes no attempt in the play to deal with anything deeper than the polite surfaces of life. The heroine's rebellion is not serious, and in the upshot, after receiving much worldly advice about bowing the neck as well as the knee to Mrs. Grundy, (to whom the preface is dedicated), she is consoled by her errant husband's promise to take her to Bond Street and buy her all the jewels she desires.

Michael and His Lost Angel *Michael and His Lost Angel* (1896) was a more courageous attempt to treat a serious subject seriously. It was "booed" by a first-night audience at the Lyceum, and, to quote the author, "again I met with the general condemnation of the press;" it was equally a failure in New York. In the author's and his editor's opinion, it is the highest of Jones's achievements; but if it failed at the time because it was too much in advance of public opinion, it failed to secure the respect of the next generation because the problem was not faced with sufficient courage on the part of the dramatist. The forward-looking eye of Bernard Shaw marked this at the time, and the dramatist himself acknowledged defeat by returning to polite comedy, dealing only with the surfaces of life, such as *The Liars* (1897) and *Mrs. Dane's Defence* (1900), excellent in their superficial way, but attempting nothing beyond the provision of a conventional evening's entertainment. *The Lie* was put

on the New York stage in 1914, but did not reach London *The Lie*
till 1923, with Sybil Thorndike in the leading part. At
the latter date it was cruelly stigmatized by James Agate
as "in the manner of 1860." "This is the old world where
strong men are fearful of meeting one another, or even
their womenfolk, face to face, and prefer the postman;
where a hero, who can be trusted to dam the Nile single-
handed, has to have his love affairs managed for him by
somebody else; where men of engineering genius, who would
not take thrust or pull on trust, believe incredible things
of a fiancée at the merest whisper."

"The 1860 manner" is hyperbole, but it is none the less
true that Jones, in spite of valiant efforts, never succeeded
in shaking himself free from the dramatic technique and
the point of view of the earlier Victorian period in which his
first efforts at dramatic composition were made.

IV. ARTHUR WING PINERO (1855-   )

Sir Arthur Pinero was more fortunate than H. A. Jones, **Pinero's**
not only in being born at a later date in London, but in **early stage**
passing before he was twenty from his father's law office **experience**
to the stage; varied experience in London and the provinces
as an actor, including a five years' engagement with Irving
at the Lyceum, gave him a familiarity with the conditions
of theatrical production which served him in good stead
during a career of dramatic composition extending well on
toward half a century.

Pinero's versatility was as remarkable as his stagecraft,
and, beginning to produce in 1877, he had put a score or
so of plays to his name before a successful plunge into mid-
Victorian sentiment (*Sweet Lavender*, 1888) gave him
fame and fortune and left him free (to use his own phrase)

"to write great plays regardless of the predilections of the public." His first attempt in this laudable crusade was apparently *The Profligate* (1889), which deals somewhat superficially with the punishment of a dissolute man about town who has married an innocent schoolgirl, not, as one might expect, by his disappointment in the schoolgirl, who turns out all that his fancy painted her, but in the unfortunate recurrence of another lady who turns up persistently at railway stations and Italian villas with protestations about outraged virtue. One can hardly take this play seriously, because the author himself did not take it seriously. After condemning the profligate to suicide in the original version, he accepted the suggestion of John Hare, the actor-manager who produced the play, and let the sinner off with a happy ending. So that instead of being a reproof of vice, the play, as acted, was really an encouragement of it, and the profligate, instead of being a horrible example, suggested rather the possibility of making the best of both worlds.

We had better accept (at any rate so far as Pinero is concerned) the assurance of the editor of his collected plays, Clayton Hamilton, that the modern English drama began when *The Second Mrs. Tanqueray* was acted for the first time on the stage of the St. James's Theatre in London on May 27th, 1893. We should pay heed to his further remark that Pinero was encouraged to compose the play "by the exhibition of Ibsen's *Ghosts* in London in 1891." Clayton Hamilton also reminds us, and it is a useful reminder, that while the impulse to write a serious play, dealing seriously with a serious subject, came to Pinero from Ibsen, Pinero did not take over the Ibsen technique. He contented himself with the easier and more

The Profligate

The Second Mrs. Tanqueray

34

theatrical manner devised by Scribe and improved by Dumas.

The Second Mrs. Tanqueray made a success beyond the author's expectation, partly owing to the successful acting of Mrs. Patrick Campbell as the wicked heroine, and partly owing to the fact that Pinero was not so much in advance of his public as he thought. His subsequent experience and that of the younger men who came later, (whether they followed in his footsteps or not is another question), showed that by this time the British public, or at any rate a small section of it, had become sufficiently educated to appreciate this kind of play.

What kind of play is it? Well, in the first place, it is a play presenting an idea or thesis or problem, though not a very involved or weighty one. Aubrey Tanqueray has taken as his second wife a lady, one can hardly say of doubtful reputation, for her reputation was beyond all doubt. She has led a life of open irregularity, not merely with one man, but with several, and Aubrey Tanqueray knows when he marries her that she will not be received by his friends. The progress of the play shows not merely the impossibility of their social position, but the impossibility of his wife's domestic position, especially in relation to his innocent young daughter, who, immediately on her release into the world, falls in love with a young officer who has previously conducted a liaison with her stepmother. Paula, on the eve of her marriage, had offered her husband a complete list of her various intrigues, but he had generously burned it without reading it, and it is she who prevents the marriage of Captain Ardale to her step-daughter by the revelation of his previous relation to herself. After this she commits suicide, but these three actions are the only evidence of uprightness or even of common sense shown by Paula Tanqueray in the course of the play. Otherwise she is neurotic, ill-tempered, with none of even the superficial attraction which women of the upper ranks of her profession are supposed to exercise. When (after staying away for two months, it is true,) one of her husband's former friends—an influential married lady living near—is induced to make the necessary social advance of calling, Paula shows quite inexcusable ill-temper and rudeness; and her husband begins to see, a little late in the day perhaps, that he has not acted wisely in bringing his young and innocent daughter into contact with "poor Paula's light, careless nature."

Now of course it is excellent morality that the leopard cannot change her spots, and that a woman who has once led an irregular life will remain forever after absurdly jealous, incapable of controlling herself or even of exercising her wits for her own advantage, but is it true? There is general agreement, even on the French stage, which is more liberal than ours in these matters, that the lesson Pinero wishes to teach is a sound one, and that it is an act of supreme folly for a man to attempt to project into regular society a lady whose life has been notoriously irregular. The trouble with Pinero's presentation is not that it is unconvincing, but that it is too convincing. It proves too much, and offers a painful contrast in this respect with several treatments of the same theme on the French stage by Augier and others, and with the very different treatment of the same issue in fiction by Meredith in *One of our Conquerors*. In the latter novel, the lady, although in an irregular position, is entirely sympathetic, but she is unable to overcome the defects of her social position and breaks under the strain. In Pinero's play the lady is entirely unsympathetic. She has absolutely nothing and does absolutely nothing to commend herself to us. In fact she brings her fate entirely on her own head, everybody else having acted with the greatest possible consideration for her.

The claim made by Clayton Hamilton and other admirers of Pinero that this is the first masterpiece the English stage can show after the production of *The School for Scandal* in 1777 is one that cannot be accepted. It is true the play made a great sensation in England at the time, but if it is put to the test of continental standards, it must be admitted that in subject, in thought, and in technique, it was already old-fashioned at the time it was written, and the lapse of years has served only to reveal its essentially conventional trivialities.

From the technical point of view the action is well devised according to the traditions of the well-made play. The author has selected a number of possibilities and combined them ingeniously so as to provide effective stage situations. Granted a man foolish enough to marry a woman of Paula's character, it is possible that his young daughter, who has hitherto stayed away from him, should propose to return to him (end of Act I); it is possible that having returned, she should not get on well with her stepmother, and that she should be sent away to Paris; it is possible that the first man she meets there should be one of her stepmother's old lovers and that she should fall in love with him; it is possible that they should all return to her home and that they should arrive unannounced; it is possible that the stepmother would reveal to her husband her former relation to the young officer to whom her stepdaughter is engaged, and that having revealed it, she would commit suicide; all this is possible, but it is far from inevitable; it is hardly probable, though perhaps it is probable enough for the purposes of an evening's entertainment on the stage. It is, of course, inevitable that Paula Tanqueray should be unhappy in her enforced seclusion; it is inevitable that her husband should be unhappy with her; but the engagement of her former lover to her stepdaughter is invented for the purposes of the play to bring about a conventional ending of suicide. The treatment by means of the older Scribe technique of a subject no doubt suggested by Ibsen is fatal to the permanent reputation of the play as a work of art. It is a transition play and is only of interest from that point of view.

Pinero within the play never showed the slightest reason for his original assumption—that Aubrey Tanqueray would marry a woman not merely of Paula's reputation but of Paula's character. Why should he? He makes no pretence of a mad passion; he is between forty and fifty, a man with a daughter almost grown up (nineteen) and with a knowledge of the world; he describes his feelings for Paula as "a temperate, honourable affection," and looks forward to a life of happiness and good repute, though he admits he is building on a miserable foundation. Evidently the justification for the marriage was to be provided by the personal charms of the actress taking the part, and Pinero was excellently served by Mrs. Patrick Campbell, an actress of admirable talent and fashionable reputation. She made the play and gave it such verisimilitude as it possesses.

The Notorious Mrs. Ebbsmith

Pinero tried again two years later (1895) in *The Notorious Mrs. Ebbsmith*, which was evidently written for Mrs. Patrick Campbell. The character was a more ambitious undertaking, both for actress and playwright, and Pinero told Clayton Hamilton that he considered Mrs. Ebbsmith the most interesting woman he had created. She is a young widow who has made herself prominent in

Socialistic agitation and has earned the nickname of "mad
Agnes." After a career of severe hardship she has taken
refuge in a hospital and from being a patient has become
a nurse—a transition which is glossed over rather too
easily. As a nurse she rescues from a severe illness a young
English M. P., a grass widower who has been travelling on
the Continent, and they have set up house together at
Venice. His wife and his relatives come to Venice and urge
him to conduct his amours with greater discretion for fear
of injuring his public career. The interest of the play
lies in the efforts of Agnes Ebbsmith to defeat the attempt
to detach her lover from her—which she at first succeeds in
doing—and in her failure to maintain their free union on
the high level she has planned. She has in mind for the
future an intellectual comradeship, devoid of passion, in
which they would work together openly for the regenera-
tion of humanity. He wants to eat his cake and have it—
to enjoy her personal charm and the solace of her com-
panionship and to keep his old place in the world. For a
while, she yields for the sake of keeping him, but ultimately,
after throwing the Bible into the fire, she drags it out again
and takes refuge in the household of a clergyman to pray
for the husband she has misled, and the wife she has
wronged. This idea does not occur to her—or to anyone else—till the very end of the play, and her repentance
is so contrary to common experience of Socialistic ladies
who console deserted husbands that the public rather
sniffed at it. The repentance was too sudden and too complete to be convincing.

In the same year was produced *The Benefit of the Doubt*, *The Benefit of the Doubt*
but in this there was no question of doing anything but
covering up the indiscretion of a married lady who had
been too frank under the influence of two glasses of cham-

pagne. A benevolent bishop was introduced in the last act to take the erring lady under his social wing, and as it is merely a question of saving her face, all ends happily.

After a play or two written in what Clayton Hamilton calls Pinero's "vacational intervals," in which he "rests his inventive mind," the author stiffened his intellectual sinews for the problem of *The Gay Lord Quex* (1899)—acted with enormous success by John Hare and Irene Vanbrugh both in London and New York and successfully revived in 1917-18. It is undoubtedly a very cleverly devised play; its bedroom scene, around which the whole structure is built, is perhaps the very best of bedroom scenes, and might have been thought to exhaust that particular situation if the experience of the New York stage since the revival had not been to the contrary. But, except as an evening's entertainment, the play has no interest and no significance. The only question at issue is whether the old roué Quex will succeed in marrying the silly little society girl he has set his heart on, and except as a sporting proposition this issue is of no possible interest to anyone. The characters exist only for the sake of a very cunningly devised situation—the bedroom scene—and when this is over the play is done. It was worth the money as an intellectual excitement when it was new, but one cannot imagine anybody wanting to see it—must less to read it—twice. Yet in the opinion of many critics it shows Pinero at his best—*i. e.,* exercising to perfection his peculiar talent.

Pinero's plan of making a play is, according to his own statement, to imagine his characters and then construct the plot, but one can hardly believe that *The Gay Lord Quex* was built by this method. In no play up to this point had Pinero taken a character and allowed him—or her—to work out an inevitable destiny. He always interposes the long

The Gay Lord Quex

40

arm of coincidence in order to make the clash more obvious and effective. His next play *Iris* (1901) has been put for- *Iris* ward by his admirers as fulfilling the exacting requirements of permanent art, but it does not do so altogether and on the stage it was not a success. It is, however, an eminently readable play if we make the author a few concessions. Iris Bellamy is a young widow whose late husband has left her a fortune which she loses if she marries— not an altogether unenviable position, some might think— but she is of a soft, luxurious, self-indulgent nature, and her natural inclination to remarry is divided between a young amateur artist (Trenwith) without a penny, whom she is fond of, and a rich Jewish financier whom she finds only just tolerable. We first see her at a dinner party at her own house, at which she has accepted the millionaire Maldonado, but after the party is over she feels he is impossible and withdraws her word in order to take the young artist abroad with her as her lover—in secret, for if he is openly her lover, he must go off to British Columbia to earn a living for both of them in lieu of the forfeited inheritance. They are still living in a fool's Paradise on the Italian Lakes when the inheritance conferred by the dramatist upon the heroine is lost by the dishonesty of her trustee, and her lover goes to British Columbia accordingly, while she retires to an obscure pension to live on her small remaining income in the meantime. Maldonado, piqued at his rejection and angry at her acceptance of young Trenwith, cloaks his passion under the guise of friendliness, and induces her to accept financial help, which, with her habitual extravagance, she soon finds insufficient. She realizes her dependence on him and makes a despairing effort to get on without it. In her lowest straits he offers her a refuge—on conditions—and she becomes his mistress.

They are unhappy together, but he is still attached to her and offers to make her his wife. She is half inclined to accept, but asks for a week's respite in the hope of her lover's return from British Columbia. And of course he does return—that very evening. Iris receives him at her flat—Maldonado's flat—tells him her story, and he leaves her for ever, though the log-hut in British Columbia is now ready for its occupants. But the meeting has been suspected and watched by Maldonado, who, mad with jealousy and rage, bursts in upon the deserted woman to turn her with brutal violence out of her last refuge into the street. William Archer said (and it appears probable) that Pinero intended to end the play with Maldonado throttling Iris, but he eventually decided on the preferable expedient of turning Iris out and rang the curtain down on Maldonado smashing up the furniture of the flat. In spite of some minor improbabilities and coincidences *Iris* is the best of Pinero's serious plays. It is a conscientious and artistic study of character, exhibiting the ruin of a weak and vacillating woman under the stress of circumstance. If Iris had the courage to marry Maldonado in the first instance or to share Trenwith's poverty in British Columbia, she would doubtless have been unhappy, but she would not have come to irretrievable ruin. She was right in thinking that she was unfitted for anything but a life of luxury; if she could have combined love with it, she would doubtless have been a model wife and a very successful hostess. It may be that the virtue of other successful hostesses and model wives stands on no more secure foundation, and that we take them for what they are because they have not been tried. They are the more fortunate on that account, but we cannot waste any bitter tears on Iris, who, after all, gets only what she deserved. As a rule, things have to be paid for in this life, and the lesson of the play, if somewhat obvious, is a wholesome one.

Pinero's later work would hardly seem worthy of detailed examination if it were not for the extravagant claims made by his admirers on its behalf. Clayton Hamilton, writing in 1922, claims that *The Thunderbolt* and *Mid-Channel* may be regarded as "the two greatest plays of British authorship that have been given to the world in the first two decades of the twentieth century." Technically, he considers *The Thunderbolt* "the ultimate monument of intensive artistry in the modern drama" and "is willing to risk the statement that *Mid-Channel* is a greater play than *Hedda Gabler* or *A Doll's House.*" This is certainly a tremendous risk, and Mr. Hamilton is on safer ground when he claims that these two plays represent Pinero's mind "at its most completely characteristic moment." Pinero, he reports, wrote them "to please himself," and was not taken aback when the English public failed to appreciate them. *The Thunderbolt* presents itself as a study in provincial life: four families are offered for our inspection, James Mortimore and his wife, Stephen Mortimore and his wife, Thaddeus Mortimore and his wife and children, Rose Ponting (*née* Mortimore) and her husband; they are all eager to divide the estate of their deceased brother Edward, and to do as little as possible for his illegitimate daughter, Helen Thornhill. As he appears to have died intestate, Helen is at their mercy until it is disclosed that Mrs. Thaddeus Mortimore has secretly destroyed, just before Edward's death, a will in which he left his fortune to Helen Thornhill, who thereupon offers to divide the estate with them in equal shares. Apart from the excitement of a well-constructed plot, the interest of the play lies in the revelation of the small-mindedness of these petty

43

provincial magnates, their jealousies and snobberies, and the contrast between their hectoring attitude to Helen when they have the whip hand of her and their cringing when it becomes clear that she has the whip hand of them. Only in the case of Thaddeus and his wife does Pinero allow any alleviation of the dark colours in which he paints English provincial society; James and Stephen are monsters of greed, hypocrisy, and vulgarity; Colonel Ponting and his wife add to these vices a foolish pretentiousness. As a representation of contemporary English society claiming historical accuracy they are absurd. Clayton Hamilton chooses this play as the best example of Pinero's power to "distinguish the natural key of unpremeditated conversation from the more formal key of studied and premeditated prose." Well, as a sample of the "unpremeditated conversation" of a little girl, take the following consecutive utterances of Joyce Mortimore, interrupted only by the exclamations of Helen:

Grandfather was a grocer, Helen—a grocer. Oh, mother has suffered terribly through it—agonies. We've all suffered. Sometimes it's been as much as Cyril and I could do to keep our heads up; but we've done it. The Singlehampton people are beasts. If it's the last word I ever utter—beasts. And only half of it was grocery—only half. It was a double shop. There were two windows; the other half was bottles of wine. They forget that; they forget that!

In the same scene the curate invites the ladies to go out in these terms:

Ladies, I have reason to believe that several choice specimens of the *Dianthus Caryophyllus* refuse to raise their heads until you grace the flower-show with your presence.

This might be defended as the curate's "premeditated prose," but his off-hand conversation (and he is a "sympathetic" character, obviously intended to pair off with the heroine in good time) is in much the same tone:

My dear Miss Thornhill, to show you how little I regard myself as worthy of the privilege of lecturing you; to show you how the seeds of selfishness may germinate and flourish even in the breast of a cleric—may I make a confession to you. I want to confess to you that the circumstances of your having been left as you are—cast adrift on the world, unprotected, without means apart from your own talent and exertions—is one that fills me with—hope.

This is not the conversational style of any provincial curate; it is the stage style of Sir Arthur Pinero.

Mid-Channel, as interpreted by Ethel Barrymore in the United States, ran for over a year, but in London, even with the valiant help of Irene Vanbrugh, it was much less successful, both at its original production in 1909 and on its revival in 1922. It is amusing to contrast the verdict of a London critic (Sydney W. Carroll) on the latter occasion, with the encomiums of Clayton Hamilton, quoted above and penned about the same date—"only so much lumber of the past . . . a muck-heap of drawing room débris . . . There are other ways of making people suffer *mal de mer* than through marriage. Watching comedies like this is one of them." The "theme" of the play (again to quote Clayton Hamilton, "eternally important to every member of the theatre-going public") is the folly of people who marry with the determination not to have any children. The wife consoles herself with a collection of "tame robins," and when she becomes so much entangled with one of these that she loses both her husband and her lover, she commits suicide. Husband and wife are alike in their lack of ordinary respect for themselves or each other, their manners are even worse than their morals, and one would be

Mid-Channel

sorry for any children committed to their charge; it would have ruined the children without saving the parents. In spite of the deep human issues involved, the play deals entirely with the superficies of life, and the wordy sermons of the conventional *raisonneur*, Peter Mottram, are insufferably tiresome. This character is, as Sydney Carroll puts it, a warning to the younger generation against the folly of "allowing interfering old gentlemen to make themselves such conspicuous nuisances, giving advice and passing observations that can only lead to the discomfort and suicide of the people to whom they are given."

Summary   Pinero is little more than a skilful stage craftsman, admirable as a contriver of a lively drawing-room comedy, but holding no permanent place in dramatic literature. He is well worth study by those who seek to acquire familiarity with the technical devices of the modern stage; he has nothing to say to those who look to the drama for a revelation of human life and character by artistic means. Professor Ludwig Lewisohn's judgment upon him, though undoubtedly severe, is just: "His is a conventional mind under the impact of a world in the throes of moral protest and readjustment; his, a conventional technique under the impact of a nobler and a plainer art. In the direction of that finer art his progress has been less than moderate. With the intellectual dilemma he has dealt by pleading for certain exemptions from the full rigour of the social law. Except in *Iris* he has always treated the problem of sex as one of social, rather than of personal, reality and conflict. In that emphasis upon the external social order his art is akin to that of the French stage, but he lacks the latter's passion, its keen intelligence, its conviction, and its style. The extraordinarily high position which he holds in the world of the English drama is sure to decline rapidly with the introduction of such critical standards as are unhesitatingly applied in every other department of imaginative literature."

V. OSCAR WILDE (1854-1900)

Oscar Wilde was a phenomenon whose significance belongs rather to literary history than to the exposition of the development of modern English drama. As the leader of the decadent school of the naughty 'nineties, his work attracted an amount of attention which was out of all proportion to its merits, or even its demerits, and the scandal of his fall, which for a time put a ban on the production of his plays, after a while enveloped the author's personality with a kind of satanic aura.

Of his romantic dramas, the only one which demands even passing mention is the one-act *Salomé*, originally *Salomé* written in French and extraordinarily successful in Germany, where Richard Strauss used it for the libretto of his opera, now better known than the original play. The four comedies, all produced between 1892 and 1895, are brimful of epigram and paradox, and no doubt helped to brighten the dialogue of the drawing-room plays of the next two or three decades. The first three are marred by shallow and tawdry sentimentalism, and the characters are often as lacking in humanity as the episodes are lacking in probability. One of Wilde's favourite epigrams was: "The first duty of life is to be as artificial as possible," and he seems to have conceived this as also the first duty of the dramatist. But his comedies have kept the stage, and it is impossible to overlook them altogether in estimating the factors which contributed to the revival of English drama at the end of the nineteenth century.

It would be futile at this date to point out the improbabilities and inconsistencies of *Lady Windermere's Fan* or
the impudent unnaturalness alike of its characters and its
dialogue. It was an old-fashioned play when it was born,
and contemporary critics were quick to point out its glar-
ing imperfections. The veteran nineteenth century critic
of the London drama, Clement Scott, writing in the *Daily
Telegraph* immediately after the first performance at St.
James's Theatre, said: "The story is of the slightest
consequence; plot, intrigue, interest, are beneath his
consideration; character-painting, creation, and development result in an amusing crowd of Oscar Wildes . . . .
The play is a bad one, but it will succeed. No faults of
construction, no failure in interest, no feebleness in motive,
will weigh in the scale against the insolence of its carica-
ture." On the first performance in New York the critics
were equally prompt in condemnation. The *Herald* said:
"It is ingeniously constructed; it is sufficiently supplied
with striking situations; it is written in fluent and often
pungent dialogue, and it moves steadily and rapidly to a
climax. The form of it manifests artistic talent and pleases
the sense of symmetry. At that point its worthiness ceases.
The substance of it is false and the spirit of it is pert. No
such persons exist as those that populate its scenes, nor is
there anywhere such a state of society extant as Mr. Wilde
has suggested. The characters are a hybrid collection and
the plot a rigmarole of impossible incidents." Wilde
affected to despise newspaper criticism, and he was annoyed
by the suggestion that the change at the end of Act I by
which he let the audience into the secret of Lady Windermere's relationship to Mrs. Erlynne at an earlier point in
the play than he had originally intended, was owing to
newspaper comment. His letter to the *St. James's Gazette*

at the time is a characteristic production and is worth quoting:

> Allow me to correct a statement put forward in your issue of this evening to the effect that I have made a certain alteration in my play in consequence of the criticism of some journalists who write very recklessly and very foolishly in the papers about dramatic art. This statement is entirely untrue and grossly ridiculous.
>
> The facts are as follows. On last Saturday night, after the play was over and the author, cigarette in hand, had delivered a delightful and immortal speech, I had the pleasure of entertaining at supper a small number of personal friends; and as none of them was older than myself, I naturally listened to their artistic views with attention and pleasure. . . . All my friends, without exception, were of the opinion that the psychological interest of the second act would be greatly increased by the disclosure of the actual relationship existing between Lady Windermere and Mrs. Erlynne—an opinion, I may add, that had previously been strongly held and urged by Mr. Alexander.
>
> As to those of us who do not look upon a play as a mere question of pantomime and clowning, psychological interest is everything, I determined, consequently, to make a change in the precise moment of revelation. This determination, however, was entered into long before I had the opportunity of studying the culture, courtesy, and critical faculty displayed in such papers as *The Referee, Reynolds'* and *The Sunday Sun.*

With the exception of *The Importance of Being Earnest*, none of the Wilde plays had a "good press;" the author ascribed it to the fact that in one of his stories he had made a character say: "All the dramatic critics are to be bought, but to judge by their appearance they cannot be very expensive." The real reason of the critical condemnation of Wilde lay, of course, in the plays themselves, and not in any personal quarrel with the dramatist, whose conviction and imprisonment while *The Importance of Being*

The Importance of Being Earnest

Earnest was still in its first London run led to the disappearance of his name from the playbills, though not to the disappearance of the play from the boards of the St. James's Theatre. The professional critics were irritated by the careless craftsmanship of the earlier comedies, their insolent admixture of sentimentalism and cynicism, their superficial glitter, and the evident contempt of the author for both the theatre and the audience. They praised *The Importance of Being Earnest*, because, though its plot and characters are obviously absurd, there is more in it of the genuine Wilde which lay behind all his poses. Max Beerbohm, speculating, some years after Wilde's fall, on the loss to the stage incurred by his disgrace, wrote in the *Saturday Review* (November 26, 1904):

> His mind was essentially a fantastic mind. Into his last play, *The Importance of Being Earnest*, he poured much of this essence, treating the scheme of a commonplace farce in an elaborately fantastic spirit, and thus evolving an unrelated masterpiece which has often, and never passably, been imitated. I fancy that his main line of development would have been from this play. Abandonning the structure of commonplace farce, he would have initiated some entirely new kind of fantastic comedy—comedy in which the aim would have been not to represent men and women, but to invent them, and through them to express philosophic criticisms of the actual world.

St. John Hankin, in a *Fortnightly Review* article published in May, 1908, came to a similar conclusion:

> Paradoxical as it may sound in the case of so merry and light-hearted a play, *The Importance of Being Earnest* is artistically the most serious work that Wilde produced for the theatre. Not only is it by far the most brilliant of his plays considered as literature. It is also the most sincere. With all its absurdity, its psychology is truer, its criticism of life subtler and more profound, than that of the other plays. And even in its technique

it shows, in certain details, a breaking away from the conventional well-made play of the 'seventies and 'eighties in favour of the looser construction and more naturalistic methods of the newer school.

These judgments have been borne out by the subsequent history of the comedies on the stage. When *The Importance of Being Earnest* was revived at the Actors' Theatre, New York, in May, 1926, it was noted that the play had more life in it than its predecessors, carelessly built on a combination of the models of Sheridan and Scribe. Wilde had considerable dramatic gifts, but he lacked the will power to make the best of his talents. He wanted money, and he saw in the play an opportunity of making it by an exercise of his turn for epigram; this, combined with a large dose of sentimentalism, which was as insincere as the small dose of cynicism was genuine, and an insolent borrowing of old stage tricks, was enough to win a temporary success; it was not enough to win critical approval or to ensure a permanent place for his work in dramatic literature. His contribution to the development of English comedy was confined to the encouragement of the Sheridan tradition of sparkling dialogue; his influence on the artistic form and social or intellectual significance of the drama was exceedingly slight.

PLAY LISTS

Principal plays only are cited

T. W. ROBERTSON

1864 *David Garrick.*
1865 *Society.*
1866 *Ours.*
1867 *Caste.*
1869 *School.*

W. S. GILBERT

1875 *Trial by Jury.*
1877 *The Sorcerer.*
1878 *H. M. S. Pinafore.*
1880 *The Pirates of Penzance.*
1881 *Patience.*
1882 *Iolanthe.*
1884 *Princess Ida.*
1885 *The Mikado.*
1887 *Ruddigore.*
1888 *The Yeomen of the Guard.*
1889 *The Gondoliers.*

H. A. JONES

1882 *The Silver King* (with Henry Herman).
1884 *Saints and Sinners.*
1889 *The Middleman.*
1890 *Judah.*
1891 *The Dancing Girl.*
The Crusaders.
1894 *The Masqueraders.*
The Case of Rebellious Susan.
1896 *Michael and His Lost Angel.*
1897 *The Liars.*
1900 *Mrs. Dane's Defence.*
1913 *Mary Goes First.*
1914. *The Lie.*

A. W. PINERO

1885 *The Magistrate.*
1888 *Sweet Lavender.*
1889 *The Profligate.*
1893 *The Second Mrs. Tanqueray.*
1895 *The Notorious Mrs. Ebbsmith.*
1898 *Trelawney of the "Wells".*
1899 *The Gay Lord Quex.*
1901 *Iris.*
1903 *Letty.*
1906 *His House in Order.*
1908 *The Thunderbolt.*
1909 *Mid-Channel.*
1911 *Preserving Mr. Panmure.*
1912 *The "Mind-the-Paint" Girl.*
1922 *The Enchanted Cottage.*

OSCAR WILDE

1892 *Lady Windermere's Fan.*
1893 *A Woman of No Importance.*
1895 *An Ideal Husband.*
     The Importance of Being Earnest.
1896 *Salomé.*

CHAPTER III

George Bernard Shaw (1856-   )

**Shaw's
early
career**

BERNARD SHAW is beyond question the central
figure of the revival of the modern drama in England. It is difficult to say whether his reputation will
remain at the high level it has now reached, but as it has
grown slowly, there seems no reason to anticipate an
immediate decline. The story of the author's determined
struggle to make himself heard on the contemporary stage
is worth telling in some detail; the rebuffs he encountered
justified his jibe in *You Never Can Tell* (written in 1896
but not acted till 1900) that in its intolerance of modern
views the theatre of the last decade of the nineteenth century was many years behind other institutions—more
retarded even than the Church. Shaw had used both voice
and pen as a militant Socialist before he became a dramatist, and as he regarded the stage primarily as a pulpit for
the propagation of his opinions, it was not altogether
surprising that it took time for the public to realize his
genuine gift for comedy. There had to be concessions on
both sides, and Shaw had to learn to present his views in
a dramatic form which appealed to the audience's sense of
art and humour, before he was able to communicate his
message effectively.

It is Shaw's dramatic career with which we are here
concerned, and it seems unnecessary to go over the familiar
ground of his birth in Dublin of English Protestant stock,
his uneventful life there up to the age of twenty, his